TINY BATTLEFIELDS

FIGHTING CANCER

Matt Anniss

Gareth Stevens
PUBLISHING

Please visit our website, www.garethstevens.com. For a free color catalog
of all our high-quality books, call toll free 1-800-542-2595
or fax 1-877-542-2596.

Anniss, Matt.
Fighting cancer / by Matt Anniss.
p. cm. -- (Tiny battlefields)
Includes index.
ISBN 978-1-4824-1345-8 (pbk.)
ISBN 978-1-4824-1308-3 (6-pack)
ISBN 978-1-4824-1453-0 (library binding)
1. Cancer -- Juvenile literature. I. Anniss, Matt. II. Title.
RC264.A56 2015
616.99--d23

Library of Congress Cataloging-in-Publication Data

First Edition

Published in 2015 by
Gareth Stevens Publishing
111 East 14th Street, Suite 349
New York, NY 10003

© 2015 Gareth Stevens Publishing

Produced by: Calcium, www.calciumcreative.co.uk
Designed by: Simon Borrough
Edited by: Sarah Eason and Jennifer Sanderson
Picture research by: Rachel Blount

Photo credits: Cover: Shutterstock: Sebastian Kaulitzki; Inside: Centers
for Disease Control and Prevention: 42; Dreamstime: Aliced 30, Ralph
Brannan 33, Brian Chase 31, Cyberstock 26, D\'lumen 40, Jose Manuel
Gelpi Diaz 39, Dimaberkut 35, Alan Gignoux 6, Haywiremedia 45,
Mnapoli501 44, Monkey Business Images 28, Robert Semnic 27, Nikita
Sidorov 41, Spectral-design 36, Kenneth Sponsler 37, Ian Wilson 43,
Zuperpups 24; Intuitive Surgical: 29; Shutterstock: Sergei Butorin 9,
Cdrin 19, Featureflash 25, Juan Gaertner 3, 4, JeremyRichards 7, Maksim
Kabakou 16, Sebastian Kaulitzki 1, Alex Luengo 10, Mathagraphics
11, Molekuul.be 23, Monkey Business Images 15, 18, NataliTerr 20,
Nejron Photo 17, Nelik 8, Alexander Raths 22, Ljupco Smokovski 13,
Spirit of America 34, The Biochemist Artist 14, Tupungato 6, Vlue 12,
Wavebreakmedia 21; Wikimedia Commons: Simon Caulton 38,
Brian Driscoll, Vice President/Marketing, Cianna Medical, Inc. 32.

Printed in the United States of America

CPSIA compliance information: Batch #CS15GS: For further information contact Gareth Stevens,
New York, New York at 1-800-542-2595.

CONTENTS

CHAPTER 1: WAGING WAR 4

CHAPTER 2: MANY CAUSES 10

CHAPTER 3: PREVENTING CANCER 18

CHAPTER 4: TREATING CANCER 26

CHAPTER 5: THE RACE AGAINST TIME 34

CHAPTER 6: THE FUTURE 40

GLOSSARY 46

FOR MORE INFORMATION 47

INDEX 48

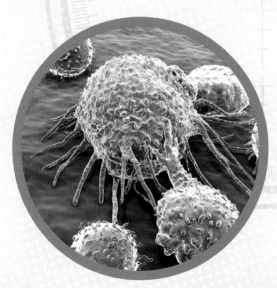

CHAPTER 1: WAGING WAR

Most people know someone who has been affected by cancer. It may be a family member who has contracted the disease or a friend who has survived it after receiving treatment. Cancer was first recorded by the ancient Egyptians in 1500 BC, and the human race has been fighting against the disease ever since. The global war against this deadly, microscopic disease is one of the longest battles in history.

A Threat to Life

Cancer is one of the biggest threats to human life around the world. Millions of people die of cancer each year, with millions more surviving after a grueling battle against the disease sometimes called "the Big C." Cancer is a truly global epidemic. It does not matter where you live, how rich you are, or how good your local hospitals are: almost anyone can contract cancer, regardless of their age or sex. Cancer is more common among older people, but certain forms of the disease can affect children and young people, too. For example, men under the age of 30 are particularly at risk from testicular cancer.

The body's natural defenses are often powerless to stop the spread of cancer cells. This illustration shows white blood cells called lymphocytes (in blue) attempting to fight a cancerous cell (in yellow).

WHAT IS CANCER?

Cancer is not a single illness but rather a very large group of diseases that are alike. Each form of cancer develops in a similar way. Normally, the human body replaces old cells with healthy new ones, but when someone has cancer, these old cells are replaced by infected, cancerous cells. Cancerous cells multiply quickly, grouping to form a tumor. If a doctor does not spot the tumor quickly, there is a chance that some cancerous cells could travel to other parts of the body and cause more tumors, increasingly the likelihood of the patient dying from the disease.

Despite great advances in recent years, scientists believe that one in every three people will get some form of cancer during their lifetime.

On the Battlefield

The United States spends more on cancer research than any other nation. Despite this investment, the country still faces a huge battle against cancer. According to the American Cancer Society, between 1.5 and 1.7 million people in the United States will get cancer every year. Of that estimate, the society believes that around 43 percent of people will die from cancer.

CANCER AROUND THE WORLD

In 2008, more than 7.6 million people worldwide died of cancer. That is around 13 percent of all recorded human deaths for that year. According to the World Health Authority, lung cancer was the third biggest killer in the world in 2011. More people die each year of cancer than other high-profile, deadly diseases such as HIV/AIDS.

FRIGHTENING STATISTICS

Also in 2008, some 12.7 million people caught one of the almost 200 different forms of cancer currently known to scientists. By 2013, that figure had leaped to 14 million. According to estimates from researchers, 48 percent of the world's cancer cases are in Asia, 25 percent are in Europe, and 19 percent in North America. Experts believe that around 47 percent of cancer cases and more than half of cancer deaths occur in less developed regions of the world. These are areas with high levels of poverty and less developed health-care systems, such as Africa, Asia, and South America. While developed nations are beginning to control cancer, the disease is more of a threat to people in underdeveloped nations than ever before.

According to the American Cancer Society, there are 14 countries in Africa without any radiation therapy facilities. This means that people with cancer in those countries cannot get the vital medical attention they need to fight the disease.

WORLDWIDE WAR

Without action, scientists predict that by 2030 there will be 30.2 million new cases of cancer worldwide every year, resulting in 13.2 million deaths. This is around 80 percent more deaths than currently occur each year. The biggest increases are likely to occur in less developed nations, where new cancer cases could increase by 81 percent— almost double the number of people with cancer in these countries today. While cancer death rates continue to slowly drop in developed regions such as the United States and Europe, elsewhere they are increasing. As a result of these statistics, in 2008, the World Health Organization (WHO) identified cancer as one of the 10 greatest threats to human health.

"Breast cancer is now a leading cause of cancer death in the less developed countries of the world. This is partly because a shift in lifestyles is causing more cases, and partly because medical advances to combat the disease are not reaching women in these regions."

Dr. David Forman, The International
Agency for Research on Cancer

Cancer rates are rising quickly in India as a result of a combination of larger urban populations, an increasingly poor diet, and unhealthy living conditions.

THE LOCATION LOTTERY

The battle against cancer is a worldwide issue, but it is of even greater significance to those in developing nations. In 2012, 57 percent of the world's cancer cases occurred in developing countries where the likelihood of dying from the disease is much greater. According to WHO statistics, around 65 percent of all cancer deaths occur in developing nations.

Cancer rates in children are much higher in developing African nations than they are in developed nations, such as the United States. Children with cancer in Africa have less chance of beating the disease than their American counterparts, too.

The Meaning of Statistics

In the United States, cancer death rates have dropped by more than 10 percent since 1999. There are similarly positive statistics for other developed nations, such as the United Kingdom, Canada, and France. Comparing the statistics of cancer deaths in developing countries to those of developed nations shows that if you live in a developing nation, you are much more likely to die from cancer than if you live in a developed nation.

Rich or Poor

While there is no one single explanation for the widening gap between cancer survival rates in rich and poor nations, money plays a significant part. Doctors in developed nations work in well-funded hospitals, have access to the latest cutting-edge treatments, and can afford to give their patients costly cancer drugs or lifesaving operations. Doctors in developing nations often do not have access to the latest scientific research, cannot offer the best treatments, and may not even have the facilities to perform operations. Even if they diagnose cancer early, there may not be a hospital or cancer clinic nearby that can treat the patient immediately. In the worldwide war against cancer, scientists must discover cures that hospitals in developing nations can afford, or persuade these nations to take greater measures to help prevent people getting cancer.

On the Battlefield

In November 2013, scientists and campaigners joined forces to urge African nations to do more to stop children dying from cancer. At the World Cancer Leaders summit in Cape Town, South Africa, it was revealed that fewer than 20 percent of African children with cancer are cured of the disease. In the developed world, more than 80 percent of children are cured of cancer. According to the experts, in Africa, cancer is either diagnosed too late or treatment is too expensive.

Since opening in 2012, the high-tech Radiological Center in Tyumen has helped save the lives of tens of thousands of cancer patients in Russia. According to statistics, 80 percent of patients make a full recovery.

CHAPTER 2: MANY CAUSES

Efforts to tackle cancer are complicated by the sheer number of different forms of the disease. At present, doctors know of more than 200 different types of cancer. Cancer is a disease that grows in body cells so it can develop in almost any type of cell, as well as in more than 60 different organs in the body.

COMMON CANCERS

The most common cancers for both sexes affect the lungs, colon, stomach, skin, and bladder. The most likely cancers to develop in women target the breasts, cervix, and ovaries, all parts of the body involved in reproduction and feeding babies. Cancers that affect men include testicular or prostate cancer.

Cancer can affect almost any part of the body, from vital organs such as the heart and lungs to bones, skin, and even blood.

Different Reasons

Cancer is particularly difficult to battle because there is no single cause or reason why a person develops cancer. Some cancers are more likely to develop because of unhealthy lifestyle choices, such as smoking or drinking too much alcohol, while others can be kick-started by environmental factors such as air pollution or coming into contact with certain chemicals. Some are even the result of a person's genes, the code inside cells that is passed down through generations.

Today, scientists understand more than ever about almost all of the different forms of cancer that affect humans. In recent years, many breakthrough discoveries into health and lifestyle habits, and their effects on the development of cancer, have helped doctors prevent or treat the disease. However, research is ongoing and there are still many things we do not understand about the disease.

"Cancer was lonely. I was bruised and hairless. And then, after a few rounds of radiation, the cancer was gone. As banged up as my body was, it was still mine. I could start putting it back in action."

Stacy Leung, breast cancer survivor

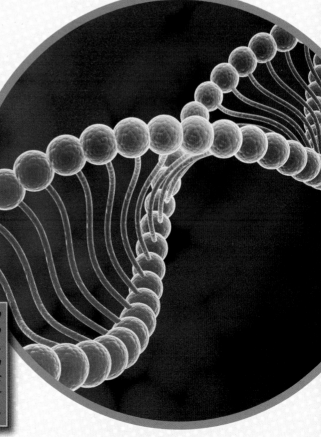

Some forms of cancer can be passed from parents to their children in their genes. Genes are contained in the "double helix" genetic code (right) at the center of every human body cell.

LIFESTYLE CHOICES

While some cancers develop with no forewarning or easily explainable cause, many are the direct result of the lifestyle choices people make every day. According to experts, one-third of people who get cancer contract the disease as a result of lifestyle choices, such as smoking, eating fatty food, being overweight, and drinking too much alcohol.

UNHEALTHY LIVING

Scientists know that smoking dramatically increases a person's chances of getting lung cancer, just as spending too much time in the sun without wearing sunscreen can result in skin cancer. Drinking too much alcohol increases the risk of getting a whole host of cancers, including those of the mouth, liver, and bowel. Not getting enough regular exercise increases a person's chances of contracting some forms of cancer, as does eating a poor diet. Scientists are even researching whether there is a link between extensive cell phone use and brain cancer.

When a person is sunburned, the damage caused to the skin can lead to genetic mutations that in turn trigger the growth of cancer cells in the skin.

NEW RESEARCH

Scientists are constantly finding new links between people's lifestyle choices and an increased risk of getting cancer. In June 2013, doctors in the United States reported an increase in young, otherwise fit and healthy women getting breast cancer.

When they looked into the causes of this alarming new increase in cancer rates, they found that most of the young women had been storing their cell phones inside their bras.

Following another recent study, the Food and Drug Administration (FDA) warned that eating french fries and other fried foods could increase a person's chances of contracting stomach cancer. This is because when food is deep fried, a chemical called acrylamide is produced. In laboratory tests on rats, the FDA found that acrylamide caused cancer. The FDA has since found significant traces of the chemical in the blood of new cancer patients whose diets are high in fried food.

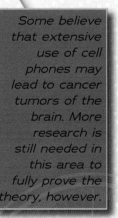

Some believe that extensive use of cell phones may lead to cancer tumors of the brain. More research is still needed in this area to fully prove the theory, however.

On the Battlefield

In the summer of 2013, researchers at the University of Minnesota revealed the results of an extensive study into the link between regular exercise and a reduced risk of getting breast cancer. They found that women who exercised at a moderate to vigorous level three times a week reduced their chances of getting breast cancer by up to 40 percent.

IN THE GENES

For many years, it was thought that lifestyle choices and environmental factors were the main underlying causes of cancer. While this is still believed to be the case in most forms of cancer, in recent years scientists have uncovered direct links between defective genes and an increased risk of developing certain forms of cancer. This phenomenon is called hereditary cancer, or cancer syndrome.

DEFECTIVE GENES

Each cell in the human body contains deoxyribonucleic acid, or DNA. DNA is the substance that stores genes, which are the traits and characteristics passed down from grandparents to parents and parents to their children. Scientists now know that some people carry defective genes that can dramatically increase the risk of getting cancer. If the DNA of a person's parents features the defective genes, it is much more likely that that person will develop cancer. Cancer syndrome explains why children whose parents or grandparents die of cancer are much more likely to develop the disease at some point themselves.

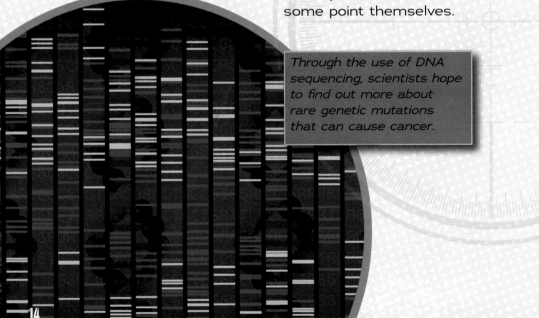

Through the use of DNA sequencing, scientists hope to find out more about rare genetic mutations that can cause cancer.

High Risk

Scientists now believe that somewhere between 5 and 10 percent of all cases of cancer can be attributed to genetic inheritance. The best-known genetic cancers are hereditary breast and ovarian cancer syndrome (HBOC) and hereditary non-polyposis colorectal cancer (HNPCC). Women with the genetic defects that cause these diseases have a 75 percent chance of developing breast, ovarian, and colon cancer at some point in their lifetime.

As scientists' knowledge of DNA and the human genome has increased, they have discovered more about the links between genes and cancer. Cancer syndrome is one of the biggest growth areas in cancer research, and it is likely that more links between certain forms of cancer and defective genes will be uncovered in coming years. Scientists are also using their increased knowledge of DNA and genetics to discover amazing new cures and cancer treatments.

"Understanding the genetic code can drive the search for targeted cancer therapies that work more effectively and efficiently. This could improve the lives of thousands of people suffering from cancer."

Dr. David J. Adams,
Wellcome Trust Sanger Institute

Gene mutations, including those that cause cancer, can skip a generation. This means that although a mother may not have a genetic mutation, her baby might.

RADIATION

All objects, however big or small, give off heat in the form of invisible waves of energy. These waves of released energy are called radiation. While most radiation is safe, some is potentially harmful. Exposure to harmful radiation can increase a person's chances of getting some forms of cancer. Scientists say that around 10 percent of cancers are caused by exposure to radiation.

CELL PHONES AND CHEMICALS

Scientists are studying the link between cell phones and cancer tumors in the brain. This is because cell phones emit radiation in the form of microwaves. If a person uses a cell phone a lot over a number of years, their chances of getting cancer may increase. There are many other forms of radiation that can cause cancer. Certain chemicals and gases, such as asbestos and radon, have been proven to cause cancer, although tumors can take up to 40 years to develop.

Cell phones emit radioactive waves of energy, even when they are in "standby" mode. Some experts believe that this could lead to an increased risk of getting cancer.

TOO MUCH SUN

One of the most common forms of cancer is skin cancer. Skin cancer, which affects around 3.5 million people in the United States every year, is caused by too much exposure to ultraviolet light. This is a form of radiation that comes from the sun and reaches Earth in two forms: UVA-A and UVA-B. Too much exposure to the latter can damage skin cells and, in time, lead to melanoma, the most dangerous form of skin cancer.

While all skin cancer is dangerous, only a small percentage of skin cancer is likely to spread to the rest of the body. According to the American Cancer Society, there are around 750,000 new cases of life-threatening melanoma in the United States every year. Experts say that skin cancer accounts for around half of all new cases of cancer in the United States every year.

In 2008, scientific research concluded that if a person gets cancer when he or she is young, it could lead to an increased risk of contracting cancer in other parts of the body, too.

On the Battlefield

In December 2013, a machine that can detect skin cancers went on sale for the first time. The device, called Aura, analyzes the body's cells underneath the skin for signs of melanoma. The machine was invented by doctors in Vancouver, Canada, and was tested for 10 years before it went on sale. To date, Aura has a 100 percent success rate in detecting skin cancers.

Chapter 3: Preventing Cancer

The fight against cancer is currently being fought on three fronts: scientific research into potential new cancer treatments, efforts to prevent people developing the disease, and successfully treating it. While research and treatment are vital, prevention is arguably the best method to cut cancer rates and keep the disease at bay.

Investing in Prevention

Cancer treatment is expensive so governments and health organizations around the world spend hundreds of millions of dollars every year on programs to help prevent people catching the disease. In 2013 alone, the US government-funded Centers for Disease Control and Prevention (CDC) spent $261 million on cancer prevention and control projects, and a further $81 million on tobacco control, much of which went toward public health campaigns to discourage smoking.

Women over the age of 50 are encouraged to go for a mammogram. This is an X-ray examination of the breasts to look for signs of breast cancer. The test is carried out every three years.

Varied Methods

Prevention programs take many forms, from discouraging people from indulging in activities that increase the likelihood of developing cancer to public health campaigns on television, radio, and in newspapers. In many wealthier nations, health-care providers are encouraged to offer patients free or low-price tests for more widespread forms of cancer, such as breast cancer, prostate cancer, and skin cancer. Information and training is also being offered to family doctors so that they can spot the warning signs of different forms of cancer at an early stage.

Changing Habits

Some hospitals and government agencies now target their efforts on the people they believe are most at risk. For example, one hospital in Poughkeepsie, New York, has decided the way to cut cancer rates is to educate at-risk families in low-income areas about the links between poor diet and cancer. In December 2013, the Vassar Brothers Medical Center hosted an event for 70 families from low-income areas at which they taught them how to cook inexpensive, healthy food in the hope that they would change their habits and stay cancer-free.

Eating too much fast food can drastically increase a person's risk of getting cancer.

"There are more than 20 million adults in this country who have not had any recommended screening for colorectal cancer and who may therefore get cancer and die from a preventable tragedy. Screening for cancer is effective and can save your life."

Tom Frieden, M.D.,
director of the CDC

LIFESTYLE AND CANCER

The first line of defense against cancer is the individual. There are a number of things people can do to either lower their risk of developing cancer or spot the early warning signs that they may have the disease.

SIMPLE LIFESAVING CHECKS

Medical experts advise women to regularly check their breasts for lumps, while men are encouraged to feel their testicles for lumps or growths. Lumps and growths can be a sign that a tumor is growing under the skin. Finding new moles or marks on the skin can also be a sign of skin cancer.

EVERYDAY CHOICES

Experts state that more than 90 percent of all cases of cancer can be traced back to lifestyle choices and the environment in which people live. Evidence collected over a number of years indicates that around 25 to 30 percent of cancer deaths occur as a result of smoking. Between 30 and 35 percent are linked to a poor diet. People can choose not to smoke and not to eat unhealthy food, which means that up to 65 percent of cancer deaths could be preventable if people simply change their lifestyle habits.

Research suggests that eliminating meat from a diet could halve the risk of certain cancers, particularly those of the stomach and bladder.

Experts say that people who exercise regularly are far less likely to get breast and colon cancer than people who do not exercise.

CHANGING HABITS

Doctors regularly advise people to exercise to help them reduce their risk of developing cancer. The likelihood of people getting skin cancer can be reduced by wearing sunscreen, covering up, and staying out of the sun whenever possible.

DIET AND CANCER

People who eat more fresh fruit and vegetables and drink less alcohol also reduce their chances of getting cancer. Much new research into the links between lifestyle choices and cancer, and in particular the foods that increase or lower the risk of developing cancer, is taking place. One day, dieticians may be able to design a diet that eradicates a person's chances of developing cancer.

On the Battlefield

Nuts are very high in fat and as a result are often thought of as unhealthy. However, a 30-year study of 120,000 Americans found that those who ate a handful of nuts every day were 11 percent less likely to die from cancer than those who did not eat nuts at all.

MEDICAL INTERVENTION

In recent years, much time and money has gone into research to find medicines that prevent people from developing cancer. While success in the area has been limited, scientists have developed some groundbreaking new medicines to keep cancer at bay and discovered that regular use of existing medicines and treatments can reduce the risk of developing cancer.

ASPIRIN AND IBUPROFEN

A study ending in 2011 proved that daily use of the common painkiller aspirin, for five years or longer, reduced the risk of contracting colorectal cancer by 7 percent and suggested a similar effect on other forms of the disease. Other common painkillers, such as ibuprofen, have also been proven to be effective in reducing the risk of developing colorectal cancer. However, these drugs are rarely used for prevention as they can cause other potentially harmful side effects, including stomach complaints.

Vaccines, which are usually injected into the body, have been successful in reducing or preventing people catching some types of cancer.

BREAST CANCER BREAKTHROUGHS

Since 2005, two drugs designed to treat patients with breast cancer, Tamoxifen and Raloxifene, have also been given to women who are at high risk of contracting the disease, as a form of prevention. Studies over the last decade suggest that if one of the two drugs is taken daily for five years, it lowers the chance of high-risk women developing

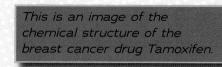

"Anastrozole provides us with another preventative treatment option, which has the potential to save and prolong the lives of millions of women."

Professor Tony Howell,
Genesis Breast Cancer charity

breast cancer by 50 percent. In 2013, another new drug designed to prevent high-risk women from developing breast cancer came into use. Women who took Anastrozole daily for five years were 53 percent less likely to develop cancer than those who did not take the drug.

CERVICAL CANCER VACCINES

Vaccines are medicines given to people to prevent them developing a disease. In many countries, children are vaccinated against common childhood diseases such as polio, measles, and chicken pox. Today, vaccines are another growth area in cancer prevention.

While success has been relatively limited in this area, since 2009, a growing number of women have been given a vaccine to prevent them developing cervical cancer. The drug Cervarix was initially designed to prevent women getting two forms of human papilloma virus (HPV), a disease that causes warts in genital/anal areas of the body and has been known to cause a rare form of throat cancer. However, Cervarix has recently been proven to decrease the risk of contracting cervical cancer by more than 70 percent. In some countries, such as South Africa, Cervarix is given to girls at the outset of puberty, while in other nations the number of teenagers having the treatment is increasing all the time. According to statistics from CDC, 33 percent of American teenage girls were given the vaccine in 2011. Experts say that it is vital that number increases in the future.

SCREENING PROGRAMS

In many developed countries, screening programs form a vital part of the fight against cancer. Screening is the process of testing people for signs of certain widespread cancers.

FINDING COMMON CANCERS

In the United States and much of Europe, women are regularly screened for signs of breast cancer and cervical cancer, and men over the age of 50 are tested for signs of prostate cancer. In 2009, a European study concluded that widespread prostate cancer screening programs reduce deaths from the disease by 20 percent.

Screening can be very successful in detecting the early signs of cancer, and, if cancer is diagnosed in the early stages, the chances of being cured increase dramatically. However, not all cancers can be detected by using screening programs, so people rely heavily on doctors being able to spot the warning signs during regular checkups.

In some countries, photofluorography machines, such as this one, are used to screen patients for signs of lung cancer.

GENE SCREEN

One of the latest developments in cancer prevention is genetic screening. This is the process of examining a person's DNA for signs of the defective genes that lead to hereditary forms of cancer. If the person is found to have the defective genes, doctors can take steps to reduce the risk of the patient developing cancer. This may include surgery to remove the body parts most at risk, such as women's breasts, or a course of cancer drugs.

To date, genetic screening tests have been developed for only a handful of hereditary forms of cancer. These include bowel, uterine, breast, and ovarian cancers. Genetic screening is an expensive and time-consuming process, so it is currently offered only to people whom doctors believe are at high risk as a result of a family history of hereditary types of cancer.

On the Battlefield

Actress Angelina Jolie made headlines in 2013 when she had both of her breasts removed after discovering that she had one of two defective genes known to cause breast and ovarian cancer. In the same year, researchers in England concluded that the action taken by Jolie, and other women with the same defective genes, drastically reduced their chances of developing breast or ovarian cancer.

CHAPTER 4: TREATING CANCER

In spite of scientists and doctors' best efforts, cancer prevention is not always successful. As a result, treating cancer and curing people of the disease is a high priority for scientists today.

No Simple Treatment

Due to the nature of the cancer, it is one of the most difficult diseases to cure. The disease can spread quickly to other parts of the body, so the success of medical treatment is reliant on doctors identifying the illness at an early stage. Even then, there is no guarantee of survival, and people with cancer face a grueling battle to rid themselves of the disease. When they do, and the cancer is in remission, they face an anxious wait to see if the disease returns in the following five years. If it does not, doctors conclude the patients have beaten the disease and can look forward to a long and healthy life.

In many cases, the first course of action when treating cancer is an operation to remove the tumor. However, this is only the first stage of treatment, and it is not always possible to cut out the tumor without causing further damage to the patient.

MEDICAL WEAPONS

A range of treatments for cancer is currently available. This includes radiation therapy and chemotherapy, surgery to remove tumors, and gene therapy. Scientists continue to research other potential lifesaving treatments, and every year new treatments are announced.

BREAKTHROUGHS

In 2013, doctors in the United States began to use a device called MarginProbe during surgery to remove tumors from patients with breast cancer. The device scans the cells around the tumor to ensure that doctors remove all of the cancerous cells, giving women with breast cancer a greater chance of beating the disease.

In another breakthrough, scientists have developed a chemical to "switch off" a defective gene called Ras, which causes one-third of all cancer tumors. Scientists at the University of California say that in laboratory tests the chemical killed human lung cancer cells caused by the Ras gene. Scientists hope that one day they will be able to turn their chemical into a lifesaving medicine, which may even be available by 2021.

On this 3D image of a pair of lungs, created using a CT scanner, you can clearly see the lung cancer tumor (marked in pink). CT scans are often used to help doctors locate cancer tumors.

"Cancers driven by Ras are the most difficult to treat. Scientists have taken a brilliantly innovative approach and have developed a strategy for targeting a mutant form of Ras with exquisite specificity."

Dr. Frank McCormick, speaking about the Ras mutant gene breakthrough

SURGERY

Cancers develop differently so different treatment methods are needed for each type of cancer. However, in many cases, the first sign of cancer growing in the body is often a tumor. This is a collection of cancerous cells that have overcome a person's natural defenses and grouped together in one area of the body. This group of cancerous cells grows quickly, replacing healthy ones. Unless it is removed, the tumor will continue to grow, and in some cases, it can spread to other parts of the body.

MALIGNANT AND BENIGN TUMORS

Tumors are not always life threatening. Those that are dangerous are called malignant tumors, while those that are not are known as benign. Benign tumors pose very little risk, but are usually removed as a standard procedure to make sure they do not become malignant in the future.

TIMING IS EVERYTHING

Whether or not a tumor can be removed from the body depends on where it is and how advanced it is. For example, removing tumors from beneath the skin can be a simple process, but surgically removing a brain tumor is hugely complex and involves a long and risky operation. Unless the cancer is so advanced that it is

Gamma knife surgery, which involves a doctor using an aluminum head frame to more accurately deliver doses of radiation, has been used to treat brain tumors and other forms of head and neck cancer since the 1990s.

inoperable (meaning that it would be too difficult to remove the tumor without causing further damage), doctors aim to operate and remove the tumor as soon as possible. When dealing with tumors, time is of the essence.

Under the Knife

In recent years, a number of advances have been made to surgical techniques that make removing some tumors easier and safer than in the past. Since 2009, some surgeons have been using a new method called robotic laparoscopic surgery to remove prostate cancer tumors. Robotic laparoscopic surgery involves using precise robotic tools, controlled by a surgeon with a computer, to open up the body and accurately remove the tumor. This cutting-edge method cuts down the risk of human error, and there are reduced side effects.

On the Battlefield

According to doctors, robotic surgery is helping to increase rates of survival in patients with lung cancer. A small cut is made in the chest. Then robotic tools, controlled by a surgeon, burrow inside the lung and remove the tumor. If the tumor removed is the size of a strawberry or smaller, doctors say that the patient has a 70 percent chance of surviving the cancer.

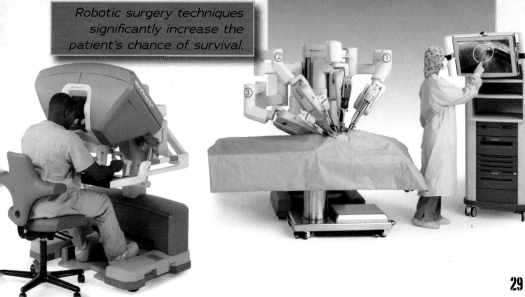

Robotic surgery techniques significantly increase the patient's chance of survival.

[CHEM]OTHERAPY

[One] of the most widely [use]d treatments in the battle against cancer is chemotherapy. It is often used on patients whose tumors are difficult to remove, or as an additional treatment for those who have undergone surgery but still have cancerous cells in their bodies.

WHAT IS CHEMOTHERAPY?

During chemotherapy, a tube is inserted into the patient's body, and a combination of anticancer drugs and powerful chemicals, such as nitrogen mustard, akyl sulfonates, and melphalan, are pumped into the patient's bloodstream. The chemicals travel around the body, killing off cancerous cells. However, many of these chemicals are so powerful that they also kill off healthy cells, leaving patients tired and sick. The chemicals can also cause patients' hair to fall out.

There is no guarantee that chemotherapy will work, but it has been proven to be very successful in curing certain types of cancer, particularly leukemia. It is sometimes also used to help people with advanced cancer live longer.

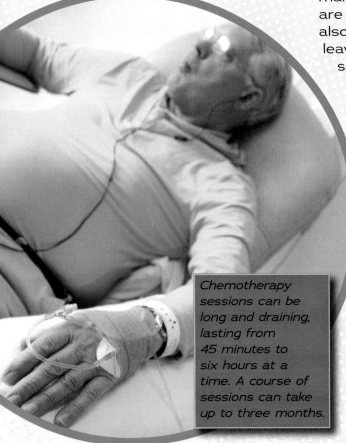

Chemotherapy sessions can be long and draining, lasting from 45 minutes to six hours at a time. A course of sessions can take up to three months.

TARGETED THERAPIES

Chemotherapy treatments have developed in recent years with scientists creating new drugs that more accurately target the molecules inside cancerous cells that lead to tumor growth. This approach is called targeted therapy, and many doctors believe that it could, in time, replace traditional chemotherapy. Targeted therapy drugs have fewer side effects, and therefore do not leave patients as tired and sick after treatment. Currently, there are targeted therapies available for a number of forms of cancer, including breast cancer, lymphoma, prostate cancer, and melanoma.

BIOLOGICS

In the future, scientists hope to discover alternatives to chemotherapy based on biologics. These are drugs based on living organisms, such as friendly bacteria of the kind that already exist in the body, which would use the power of the body's natural defenses to destroy cancerous cells.

"The very word chemotherapy generates a deep intake of breath in most people. It was a real hammer blow to be told that I would require six months of chemo. My regime consisted of eight, three-week cycles. Never has one week seemed so short. It seemed an endless grind out of my control."

James Miller, cancer survivor

One of the side effects of chemotherapy is hair loss. Many patients find that all of their hair falls out during the treatment. The hair usually grows back during recovery.

RADIATION THERAPY

Radiation therapy is one of the most common cancer treatments. It has existed in some form since Wilhelm Conrad Röntgen discovered radiation in 1895. In 1899, Emil Grubbe, a student doctor in Chicago, was the first person to use radiation to treat cancer. Three years later, two Swedish doctors used radiation therapy to cure cases of head and neck cancer. Today, radiation therapy techniques are very advanced, and there are a number of variations of therapy used to treat cancer.

WHAT IS RADIATION THERAPY?

In radiation therapy, cancer patients are subjected to doses of radiation, traditionally delivered in the form of X-rays and targeted at the area of the body affected by cancer. The radiation kills off body cells. Normal human body cells will, in time, repair themselves, while the cancerous cells die off and, hopefully, do not return.

The use of radiation therapy to treat cancer is widespread, with nearly two-thirds of cancer patients receiving the therapy at some point in their treatment. Compared to some other cancer treatments, it has a high success rate.

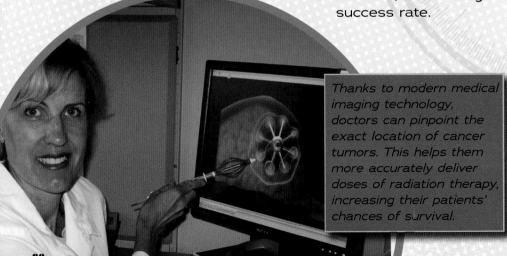

Thanks to modern medical imaging technology, doctors can pinpoint the exact location of cancer tumors. This helps them more accurately deliver doses of radiation therapy, increasing their patients' chances of survival.

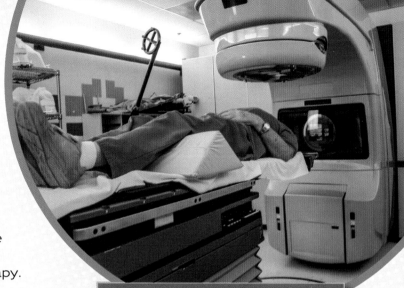

According to statistics, 40 percent of cancer survivors were treated with radiation therapy.

RECENT BREAKTHROUGHS

Radiation therapy is a tried and true treatment for cancer, so recent scientific research has focused on improving its effectiveness. One of the most recent breakthroughs has been 3D conformal radiation therapy (3DRT). In 3DRT, patients are given a CT scan to create a three-dimensional picture of the cancer tumor and its exact location inside the body. Doctors then use the image to deliver doses of radiation that accurately target the tumor.

Another important development is proton beam radiation therapy. This targets the tumor

On the Battlefield

Scientists in England have invented a new radiation therapy technique. Dynamic couch rotation volumetric modulated arc therapy (DCR-VMAT) allows doctors to simultaneously move both the beam of radiation and the table on which the patient is lying, using a computer. This way, doctors can limit the amount of radiation hitting healthy parts of the body and more accurately target tumors.

with a concentrated beam of tiny atomic particles called protons. Doctors say that proton beam radiation therapy is much more accurate than traditional methods.

CHAPTER 5: THE RACE AGAINST TIME

In 1971, President Nixon declared "war on cancer," announcing a huge boost to funding of cancer research. He hoped scientists would find cures that would ultimately lead to the total eradication of the disease. Since then, successive presidents, including President Obama, have reiterated this pledge, pouring billions of dollars into research for potential breakthroughs, experimental treatments, and cutting-edge techniques.

Barack Obama has vowed to "wage war" on cancer and fund greater research into the disease.

The Big Spend

According to government statistics, the United States government has spent more than $200 billion on cancer research since 1971. Other governments, health organizations, and charities worldwide have also spent vast amounts over the last 40 years. Cancer is a regular cause of human suffering and, in many cases, death, which is why scientists are facing a race against time to find more effective cures. With more cases of cancer being reported every year, the need for new breakthroughs is even more pressing. WHO predicts that by 2030 there could be 27 million new cases of cancer every year and 17 million deaths as a result of the disease.

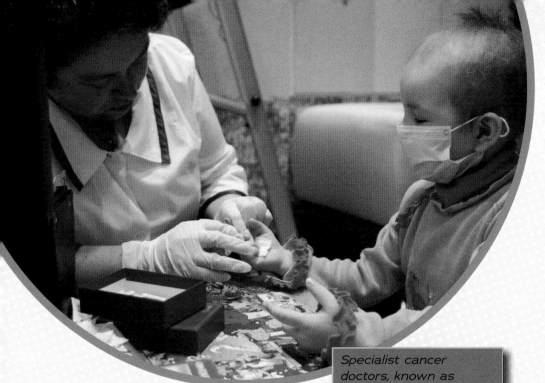

The Future, Now

The increase in funding for cancer research over the last 40 years has resulted in a number of great improvements in existing treatments, with rates of survival in developed nations, such as the United States and United Kingdom, continuing to rise. Scientists have designed medicines that cure certain rare forms of leukemia, invented targeted therapy, and made improvements to radiation therapy. Furthermore, a greater understanding of the way the human body works, particularly genes and body cells, has led to a number of exciting new treatments that are already changing the lives of millions of people suffering from cancer. These are the techniques that will be on the frontline of the battle against cancer for years to come.

Specialist cancer doctors, known as oncologists, are beginning to test the blood of children they think may be at risk of contracting cancer, in order to try to prevent them from getting the disease.

"My mother died of ovarian cancer at the age of 53. For millions of Americans, my mother's story is all too familiar. Now is the time to be waging a war against cancer as aggressive as the war cancer wages against us."

President
Barack Obama

IMMUNOTHERAPY

Since the 1990s, much cancer research has focused on a cutting-edge technique called immunotherapy. Many scientists think that immunotherapy, also sometimes called biological therapy, could one day become the most effective method of treating most forms of cancer.

This illustration shows blood cells attempting to infiltrate a virus cell. By understanding how the human immune system works, scientists can manipulate it to help battle cancer.

REPAIRING THE IMMUNE SYSTEM

The human body has a defense mechanism, called the immune system, that fights back against illness. When somebody has cancer, the cancerous cells damage the immune system and stop it fighting back against the disease. Research has shown that if the immune system is repaired, the body will naturally destroy cancerous cells.

In immunotherapy, natural substances called biological response modifiers (BRMs) are used to boost the immune system. These occur naturally in the body at very low levels, but during immunotherapy, patients are given much higher doses (usually created in a laboratory) to help their bodies battle the cancer.

Immunotherapy gives hope that even more people can overcome cancer, just like these survivors posing for photos at a fundraising event in Ohio in 2009.

"Harnessing the human immune system to target cancer could result in the development of effective treatment and potentially enhance the effect of chemotherapy."

Dr. John Morris

NEW SCIENCE

There are currently a number of different forms of immunotherapy being used to treat cancer patients. The first, known as cell immunotherapy, involves cells from a healthy immune system being inserted into a patient's body. The second, called monoclonal antibody therapy, involves drugs that boost the antibodies in the immune system that fight against disease.

BREAKTHROUGHS

Although immunotherapy is a new treatment, potentially groundbreaking developments continue to be announced every year. In 2010, the FDA approved use of a new vaccine for prostate cancer, which helps the immune system to build up a resistance to cancer. If someone who has been given the vaccine develops cancer, his or her immune system will naturally destroy it. In 2011, drug company Bristol-Myers Squibb announced that they had developed an immunotherapy medicine for melanoma that completely cured some patients, and drastically reduced the size of tumors in other patients.

Gene Therapy

Gene therapy is one of the most cutting-edge medical techniques presently used. It is still considered an "experimental" treatment, and only one form of gene therapy has been approved as safe for use worldwide.

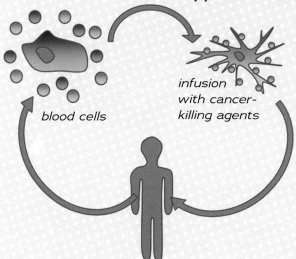

blood cells

infusion with cancer-killing agents

This diagram shows a promising new cancer treatment called dendritic cell therapy. Blood cells are removed, infused with agents known to kill cancer cells, and then reintroduced to the body.

Swapping Genes

Gene therapy involves curing someone of a disease by taking defective genes, which are buried deep in the DNA molecules at the center of each human body cell, and replacing them with healthy ones. When a person has cancer, gene therapy is used to alter their DNA, making it possible for their body to produce the healthy body cells that would naturally fight the disease.

Groundbreaking Treatment

There are currently a number of experimental studies underway with the aim of proving that gene therapy can cure some forms of cancer. In 2013, researchers at the University of Washington announced that a trial of a new form of gene therapy for treating cancers of the blood, such as leukemia, had been a success. The treatment involved filtering patients' blood so that scientists could remove millions of defective white blood cells. The cells were then altered to contain a gene that kills cancer and returned to the patients' bodies.

The treatment was tested on 27 patients who had lost all hope of being cured of their disease, including a number of young children. Miraculously, all five of the adults and 19 of the 22 children involved in the trial were completely cured of cancer. More than 120 patients have tried the treatment to date in a number of different studies, with mainly positive results.

On the Battlefield

In August 2013, scientists at the University of Pennsylvania stated that two out of three leukemia patients they had treated with experimental gene therapy had been cured. The doctors used a new form of immunotherapy T cell treatment that they hope will one day be able to cure all cases of leukemia.

More research still needs to be done before gene therapy can be used worldwide, but the success so far will give many sufferers hope.

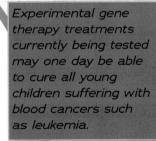

Experimental gene therapy treatments currently being tested may one day be able to cure all young children suffering with blood cancers such as leukemia.

CHAPTER 6: THE FUTURE

Although scientists and doctors have made many significant breakthroughs in the fight against cancer, the war is far from won. The battle against cancer is still greatly skewed in favor of patients from developed countries, either with government-funded health-care systems (as in some European countries such as the United Kingdom) or health insurance (as in the United States). Cutting-edge cancer treatments are very expensive (a course of chemotherapy drugs can cost up to $70,000), placing them out of reach of patients in poorer countries. Therefore, currently one of the most pressing concerns is finding cancer prevention and treatment solutions that can be used globally, by both developed and developing countries.

By closely studying the genetic makeup of cancer cells, such as this melanoma cell, scientists hope to discover new cures.

USING GENE THERAPY

Gene therapy is arguably the area of treatment with the greatest potential. As well as providing treatments for those with the disease, it may one day also be possible to treat those people with defective genes earlier in life. For example, if two parents are known to carry defective genes that cause cancer, doctors could give their children gene therapy to prevent them getting cancer in the future.

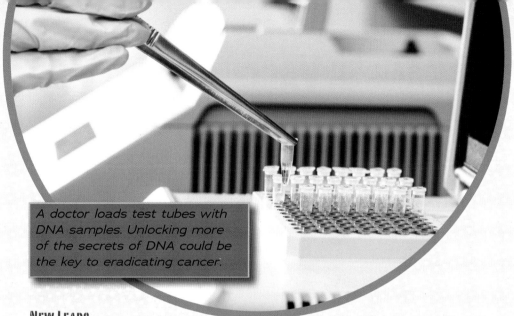

A doctor loads test tubes with DNA samples. Unlocking more of the secrets of DNA could be the key to eradicating cancer.

NEW LEADS

Many scientists around the world are currently working in the field of oncogenomics. This is the science of identifying new forms of genes that may stop the development of tumors in the body. Between them, the COSMIC cancer database and Cancer Genome Atlas projects have to date identified more than 130,000 mutations in 3,000 genes that have mutated inside cancer tumors. Experts say that most of these mutations occurred in just a few hundred genes, and it is these genes that cancer researchers will focus on in the future.

In 2010, a major report revealed that scientists had identified a number of human cell types that are instrumental in the spread of cancer in the body. Scientists say that, by focusing research on a rare type of blood cells called endothelial progenitor cells, we stand a greater chance of developing treatments that can be used against a number of forms of cancer, rather than just one.

"Our best way of understanding cancer is to understand the network as a whole and how it interacts. My prediction is that progress is going to be a lot slower than we think it might be."

Dr. Michael Gallagher, medical director of the Sparta Cancer Center

A Cancer Vaccine?

In the course of human history, many deadly diseases such as smallpox have been wiped out as a result of the development of vaccines. Already scientists are getting closer to developing vaccines to protect against deadly diseases such as HIV/AIDS, but what chance is there of scientists one day developing a vaccine that protects people against all forms of cancer?

Slow Process

Vaccines can take years to develop. Even when scientists have identified a substance, type of cell, or gene that can help boost the body's immune system, and therefore naturally fight back against a disease, they have to turn it into something that can be safely injected into the body. This means creating test versions of the vaccine in a laboratory that can be used on animals. If the results are positive, they will then start testing the vaccine on people. Even if these trials are successful, the vaccine will be tried on more people, until it is proven safe for use on the wider population. It is a very long and expensive process, costing drug companies millions of dollars. It can take between 10 and 15 years for a new drug to go from being created in a laboratory to being used regularly in hospitals.

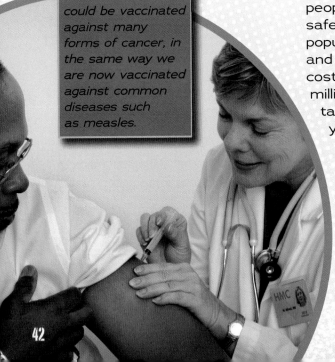

In the future, we could be vaccinated against many forms of cancer, in the same way we are now vaccinated against common diseases such as measles.

Vaccines are manufactured and transported in liquid form, ready for transfer to a syringe and injection into a patient.

REALITY CHECK

The sheer number of different forms of cancer and the varied ways they develop inside the body makes it almost impossible for scientists to produce a single vaccine that will protect against all variations of cancer. However, there is already a vaccine available that protects against prostate cancer and a drug that protects against cervical cancer. Drug companies are currently testing vaccines aimed at preventing lung cancer and breast cancer. Although the companies are hopeful these vaccines will be used in hospitals within the next 10 years, it may, in reality, take far longer.

On the Battlefield

A doctor in Cleveland, Ohio, has developed a vaccine that has successfully prevented breast cancer in mice. The vaccine, which is due to start being tested on women in 2015, boosts the immune system against the proteins found in breast tumors. That means that the body would naturally destroy cancerous cells in the breast before they form tumors.

CAN THE WAR BE WON?

The human race has been battling cancer for thousands of years and will continue to do so. Over the last century, rapid advances have been made in the prevention, treatment, and management of cancer. In the past, the chances of surviving cancer were small, but today, if the disease is spotted early enough, it is possible to be cured of most cancers.

Every year, hundreds of thousands of people whose friends and family have been affected by cancer take part in charity events in order to raise funds for further research.

PALLIATIVE CARE

If a form of cancer is not curable, it is possible to extend a cancer patient's life through a combination of cutting-edge drugs, radiation therapy, and disease management. This process is known as palliative care. In the future, it may be possible to extend cancer sufferers' lives indefinitely. Medications and treatments to extend the life expectancy of sufferers of other dangerous diseases, such as HIV/AIDS, already exist, and it is hoped that more advances in this area will be made to help cancer sufferers. Experts believe that it will not be long before cancer is a "manageable" illness.

THE BIG SWITCH-OFF

Scientists are doing everything they can to discover new cures for the disease. As they learn more about the chemical processes that lead to tumor growth, hopes increase that, one day, doctors will finally be able to "switch off" the genes that cause cancer. In the future, it may be possible to screen children at birth for cancer-causing defective genes. These faulty genes could then be replaced using gene therapy, ensuring that hereditary cancers become a thing of the past. When affected children grow up and have their own children, they would pass on healthy genes, rather than defective ones.

"It is not likely that we are going to eradicate cancer completely when it is so robust. It is much more likely that over time we are going to learn how to manage this, much as we would manage heart disease and diabetes."

Dr. Michael Gallagher,
medical director
of the Sparta
Cancer
Center

WINNING THE BATTLE

At present, a cancer-free world seems like a dream, but the pace of change over the last 100 years suggests that the dream may be possible 100 years from now. Until then, scientists will continue to work on cures and treatments to fight microscopic cancer cells in their battle against this devastating disease.

In 100 years' time, will babies be born into a cancer-free world? With continued research and medical breakthroughs, this dream may one day become a reality.

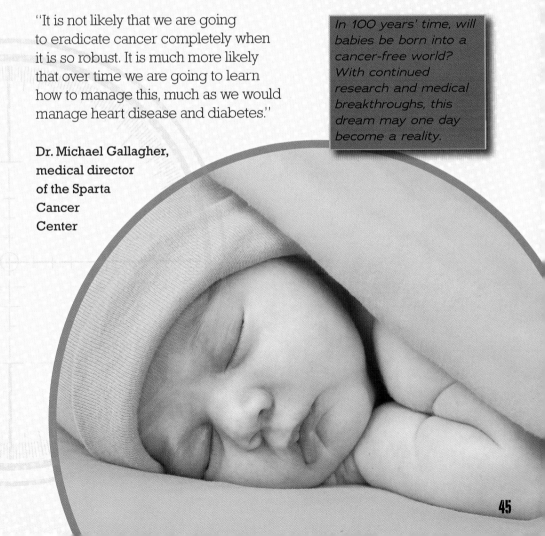

GLOSSARY

BOWEL an organ in the digestive system that processes waste matter

CANCEROUS CELLS cells that have become defective. Combined, cancerous cells form tumors

CANCER SYNDROME defective genes, passed down through families, that increase the likelihood that a person will develop cancer

CELLS the tiny units that together make up our bodies. There are billions of cells in each human body

CHEMOTHERAPY a cancer treatment that uses high doses of chemicals and drugs

COLON an organ in the digestive system that handles human waste matter

DEFECTIVE something that does not work properly or is faulty

DNA the molecule contained within each human body cell that contains our genes

EPIDEMIC a disease that is so widespread that it affects millions of people around the world

HEREDITARY something that can be passed down through families

GENES the traits and characteristics stored inside DNA

GENE THERAPY the process of altering a person's genes in order to cure them of a disease

MELANOMA a form of skin cancer

ONCOGENOMICS the study of genes and their role in cancer

ORGANS body parts, such as the lungs and heart, which do a specific task

RADIATION waves of heat and energy given off by everything in the universe

RADIATION THERAPY the process of killing cancer cells by blasting them with radiation

TUMOR a dangerous growth made up of cancerous cells

X-RAY a type of radiation

For More Information

Books

Caldwell, Wilma R. *Cancer Information for Teens* (Teen Health Series). Aston, PA: Omnigraphics Inc., 2004.

Matray-Devoti, Judith. *Cancer Drugs* (Drugs: The Straight Facts). New York, NY: Chelsea House Publications, 2006.

Walker, Julie. *Lung Cancer: Current and Emerging Trends in Detection and Treatment* (Cancer and Modern Science). New York, NY: Rosen Central, 2005.

Websites

For a concise study of cancer, log on at:
**www.eschooltoday.com/cancer/
cancer-facts-and-tips-for-kids.html**

Find out how cancer develops and how it can be treated at:
**kidshealth.org/teen/diseases_conditions/cancer/
cancer.html**

Find out more about how cancer affects teenagers and how you can make good lifestyle choices at:
www.teenslivingwithcancer.org

Publisher's note to educators and parents: Our editors have carefully reviewed these websites to ensure that they are suitable for students. Many websites change frequently, however, and we cannot guarantee that a site's future contents will continue to meet our high standards of quality and educational value. Be advised that students should be closely supervised whenever they access the Internet.

INDEX

3D conformal radiation therapy (3DRT) 33

antibodies 37

biological response modifiers (BRMs) 36
breast cancer 7, 11, 13, 18, 19, 22, 23, 24, 25, 27, 31, 43

Cancer Genome Atlas 41
cancerous cells 5, 27, 28, 30, 31, 32, 36, 42
cancer syndrome 14, 15
Centers for Disease Control and Prevention (CDC) 18, 19, 23
chemotherapy 26, 30–31, 37, 40
colon cancer 10, 15

defective genes 14, 15, 25, 27, 38, 40, 45
DNA 14, 15, 25, 38
dynamic couch rotation volumetric modulated arc therapy (DCR-VMAT) 33

Food and Drug Administration (FDA) 13, 37

gene therapy 38–39, 40, 45
genetic screening 25

hereditary breast and ovarian cancer syndrome (HBOC) 15
hereditary non-polyposis colorectal cancer (HNPCC) 15

immune system 36, 37, 42, 43
immunotherapy 36–37, 39

leukemia 30, 35, 38, 39
lung cancer 6, 10, 12, 27, 29, 43
lymphoma 31

melanoma 17, 31, 37

oncogenomics 41

prostate cancer 10, 19, 24, 29, 31, 37, 43
proton beam 33

radiation therapy 6, 11, 32–33, 35, 44

screening 19, 24–25
skin cancer 12, 17, 19, 20, 21
surgery 25, 26, 27, 28–29, 30

targeted therapy 15, 31, 35
testicular cancer 4, 10
tumor 5, 12, 16, 20, 26, 27, 28, 29, 30, 31, 33, 37

ultraviolet light 17

vaccine 23, 37, 42–43

X-rays 32